General editor: Graham Handley MA PhD

KT-196-428

Brodie's Notes on William Blake's

Songs of Innocence and Experience

Graham Handley MA PhD
Formerly Principal Lecturer in English,
College of All Saints, Tottenham

MACMILLAN

First published 1979 by Pan Books Ltd

This revised edition published 1992 by
THE MACMILLAN PRESS LTD
Houndmills, Basingstoke, Hampshire RG21 2XS
and London
Companies and representatives
throughout the world

ISBN 0–333–58051–6

Typeset by Footnote Graphics, Warminster, Wiltshire
Printed in Great Britain by
Clays Ltd, St Ives plc, Bungay, Suffolk

Contents

To the student

A close reading of the set text is the student's primary task. These Notes will help to increase your understanding and appreciation of the poems, and to stimulate *your own* thinking about them: *they are in no way intended as a substitute* for a thorough knowledge of the poems.

Preface by the general editor

The intention throughout this study aid is to stimulate and guide, to encourage your involvement in the book, and to develop informed responses and a sure understanding of the main details.

Brodie's Notes provide a clear outline of the play or novel's plot, followed by act, scene, or chapter summaries and/or commentaries. These are designed to emphasize the most important literary and factual details. Poems, stories or non-fiction texts combine brief summary with critical commentary on individual aspects or common features of the genre being examined. Textual notes define what is difficult or obscure and emphasize literary qualities. Revision questions are set at appropriate points to test your ability to appreciate the prescribed book and to write accurately and relevantly about it.

In addition, each of these Notes includes a critical appreciation of the author's art. This covers such major elements as characterization, style, structure, setting and themes. Poems are examined technically – rhyme, rhythm, for instance. In fact, any important aspect of the prescribed work will be evaluated. The aim is to send you back to the text you are studying.

Each study aid concludes with a series of general questions which require a detailed knowledge of the book: some of these questions may invite comparison with other books, some will be suitable for coursework exercises, and some could be adapted to work you are doing on another book or books. Each study aid has been adapted to meet the needs of the current examination requirements. They provide a basic, individual and imaginative response to the work being studied, and it is hoped that they will stimulate you to acquire disciplined reading habits and critical fluency.

Graham Handley 1992

The author and his work

William Blake was born on 28 November 1757, but we know very little about his family. From a very early age his capacity for seeing visions was evident: for example, at the age of eight, he asserted that he had seen a tree with angels in it. By the time he was ten he was attending Pars's drawing-school in the Strand, where his ecstatic responses to prints after Michelangelo and Dürer sent the young boy hunting for originals. He asked to be apprenticed to an engraver, and worked at his craft for two years, during which time he was sent to Westminster Abbey to make drawings for engravings. His talent was quick to reveal itself, but it was at this time that he experienced a sense of isolation. His first small volume of verse was printed in 1783, the poems having been written before he was twenty. They were, as might be expected, largely imitative, bearing the marks of some poor contemporaries as well as those of Spenser, Shakespeare and Milton. None the less there is evidence too of what Mona Wilson calls the 'self-begotten' nature of Blake's poetry, particularly among the lyrics.

At the age of twenty-two, he became a student at the Royal Academy, and was soon earning his living as an engraver. He also began to be influenced by the Swedish philosophical theologian Swedenborg. In 1782 he married Catherine Boucher, four years his junior. He taught her to write and she learned to help him in his printing and engraving; she accepted his visions and was a practical if, of necessity, frugal housewife. In 1787 Blake's beloved brother Robert died, and Blake saw his soul rise through the ceiling. He was to converse and write with the guidance of Robert's spirit for a number of years. Robert was also credited with inspiring the accompanying illustrations to his poetry. Blake would draw these up in outline on a copper-plate to be used as stereotypes. The plates could then be printed in any tint that Blake wished and either he or his wife could colour the marginal illustrations by hand in imitation of the originals. Using this new process Blake produced two tractates, *There is No Natural Religion* and *All Religions are One*. His first outstanding achievement was, however, *Songs of Innocence*, printed in coloured letters with pictures, decorations and painted text. (For the composition of *Songs of Innocence and Experience* see the section which follows this.) The first of the complex symbolic books, *Tiriel*, was written about 1789, while the second, *Thel*, approximates in mood to the *Songs of Innocence*, and is beautifully illustrated.

Allied to his mystical concepts were his strong revolutionary sympathies; he also disapproved of the conventional, legal attitude towards marriage. In the second half of 1789 he began to write a book on the French Revolution, which, however, was not published in his lifetime; it may well be that Blake himself destroyed much of what he had written after news from France of the terrible excesses (like the September Massacres) arrived in London. Blake was influenced not only by Swedenborg but also by Swedenborg's master, Jacob Boehme, the 16th-century German mystic. He returned to Swedenborg as the main inspiration when he began to write *The Marriage of Heaven and Hell*, which has been rightly called Blake's Gospel of Revolution. Written in about 1790, it is the complex record of a personal spiritual experience: it expresses Blake's belief in imaginative faith, and contains an attack on the conventional manifestations of religion. Blake believed, and his writings are sprinkled with such references, in the symbolism of the Old Testament, but he also made his own myths and symbols which would require books (there are some) of explication to provide any full commentary on his wholly individual beliefs. The symbolic books – for example, *Milton* and *Jerusalem* – contain metrical experiments far from the lyrical modes of the *Songs of Innocence and Experience*, and of course much of this reflects spiritual and auto-biographical experiences.

Blake's concept of vision takes on four dimensions, an indication of the complexity of his views; these range from simple perception, to twofold or intellectual addition, through to emotional and spiritual states. His own reference to the nature of his visionary experiences gave rise to what were, initially, theories that he was mad, or that he suffered from hallucinations. Both external perception and internal imagination applied to external objects were given to him in a kind of concentrated power, so that he could say of himself that 'I can look at a knot in a piece of wood till I am frightened of it'. But he was viewed with suspicion when he described in company what he saw: he would deliberately distort and exaggerate, probably enjoying the reactions he obtained from others. By 1791 Blake was living in Lambeth, and legend has it that on one occasion he and his wife appeared naked, having just been reading *Paradise Lost* together. At this time he was reasonably well-off: he began to take pupils and he drew a number of designs which were colour-printed. He was engaged as an illustrator for Young's *Night Thoughts*; the first part of the edition appeared in 1797 with plates engraved by Blake. In the same year he made a number of drawings for an edition of the poems of Gray while continuing to publish the prophetic books: in 1793 *America*, in 1794 *Europe* and *The First Book of Urizen*, in 1795 *The Book of Los* and *The Book of Ahania*. He had also begun to work on the long and difficult poem, *Vala*.

In 1800 Blake moved to Felpham, where he took a cottage and helped to decorate Hayley's library with the heads of famous men of literature. During this time Blake was charged with assault on a private soldier and for using seditious language: he was tried for high treason at Chichester in January 1804. The hearing was a long one, but Blake was acquitted of the charges. Both his poems

Milton and *Jerusalem* took shape during his stay at Felpham, as well as a number of his later lyrics, including the fine *Auguries of Innocence*. The preface to *Milton* contains 'And did those feet in ancient time', which was subsequently set to music and became the celebrated hymn *Jerusalem*. In the poem Blake reveals the nature of his affinity with the Puritan poet who had made an epic out of man's fall and his own adversity. Blake's *Milton* is a splendidly illustrated text, personally and idiosyncratically symbolic; the fine turns of phrase remain in the mind despite the difficulty of the whole with its passages of inflated rhetoric. Towards the end of 1803 the Blakes returned to London; shortly after, Mrs Blake became ill. Meanwhile Blake provided plates for the life of Romney and the life of Cowper, though in the case of the former another engraver was later employed.

Blake now began to experience financial difficulties, and his engraving was considered by some to be too personal to fit easily with the work of others. His engravings for Blair's *The Grave* were considered a failure, and he began advertising a series of engravings of Chaucer's Canterbury pilgrims.

Blake failed to make an impact as an artist, largely because of the strongly individual interpretation present in his engravings and paintings which did not fit into a conventional pattern. Between 1810 and 1818 there is little direct information about Blake, although there are some contemporary impressions. During this time he was writing *Jerusalem*, and probably living in near poverty and, certainly, neglect. His powers of illustration, however, had not deserted him, since *Jerusalem* contains a fine representation of the Crucifixion.

During the final period of his life Blake made a number of friends, generally among those who were much younger than he. John Linnell gave him some engraving to do because he was obviously in a bad way, and by 1820 Blake was illustrating a school edition of Virgil's *Pastorals*, which included twenty woodcuts designed by him. In 1822 he published a poem called *The Ghost of Abel*, of which only a handful of copies have survived, and between 1823 and 1826 he engraved the brilliant illustrations for *The Book of Job*, perhaps his most celebrated work. In 1825 Blake met Crabb Robinson, friend of Wordsworth and Coleridge; it was he who, when writing of Blake later, referred to the 'union of genius and madness' which was to initiate this aspect of the legend. He did, however, find in Blake 'all the elements of greatness', and his albeit limited critique is a pioneer work in Blake studies.

From 1824 onwards Blake's health began to deteriorate, though he was well cared for by the Linnells, and many of the younger artists visited him and accorded him some recognition. He continued to work on illustrations, for example for *Genesis* and the apocalyptic *Book of Enoch*. By 1827 he was in a feeble state, and he died in August. As he had said on hearing of the death of one of his friends, 'I cannot think of death as more than the going out of one room into another'. He greeted it with songs, as his wife did four years later when she went to join him.

Largely unrecognized in his own time, subjected to a life of deprivation for a while, a visionary who was thought mad by many and translucently sane by some, Blake is one of the great writers of our literature. He is also one of our great artists, a man whose signal vision appropriated both the visual and the verbal to its end. Blake believed in the transfiguring power of the imagination, and the *Songs* you are studying are, in the condensed force of their expression, his finest testimony to that power.

A critical introduction to the poems

As we have seen in the section *The author and his work*, Blake was an engraver, and he etched the plates from which his books were reproduced. The first *Songs of Innocence* contained hand-painted water-colours to accompany the poems, and a glance at these is sometimes helpful in understanding Blake's intentions; they also demonstrate Blake's dual ability, the harmonizing of the verbal and the visual in his own mind. The date on the illustrated title page is 1789, but since Blake continued to engrave and issue these hand-printed editions, the date can only be taken as a beginning; Blake adjusted and adapted as he went along, and it seems likely that some of the *Songs of Innocence* may be dated as early as 1784, while others are much later. Three versions of *Songs* included in *Innocence* are found in *An Island in the Moon*, which, according to Keynes, was written about 1784–5. In reading the later versions we must allow for Blake's development as man, poet and illustrator.

There are many critics who would insist that the *Songs of Innocence and Experience* were together conceived as an artistic whole. F. W. Bateson conveniently divides the *Songs of Innocence* into three categories which seem to this writer indisputable. First, there are those written about 1784, which are addressed to adults and which represent pastoral innocence. The next group are addressed specifically to children (*The Lamb*, *The Little Black Boy* and *The Blossom*); the influences behind their form are those of the Non-conformist hymn-writers and, more particularly, Isaac Watts. The idea of illustrating these was certainly present in Blake's mind, and they were probably written between 1784 and 1787. There is a story that after the death of his brother Robert (February 1787) Robert's spirit revealed to him the process of 'illuminated printing' (the hand-tinted water-colours referred to earlier). The third section according to Bateson consists of those poems which were later transferred to *Songs of Experience* (*The Little Girl Lost*, *The Little Girl Found*, *The Schoolboy*, *The Voice of the Ancient Bard*). These Bateson rightly calls 'sombre and more adult'.

Songs of Experience appears to have been engraved by 1793, though the copies of it which are still in existence have the date 1794 on the title page; it was probably in that year that Blake added the page which establishes the relationship between each series – 'Songs Of Innocence and Of Experience Showing the Two Contrary States of the Human Soul'. Obviously there is a gap of about five years between the two sets of engravings, but there is certainly an overlap in terms of the composition of the first and last verses in each section. The Rossetti manuscript was acquired by the poet Dante Gabriel Rossetti in 1847, and the notebook concerned was almost certainly the property of Blake's brother Robert, of whom William said, 'with his spirit I converse daily and hourly'. This notebook obviously occupied a special place in Blake's life in view of his closeness to Robert; he used it to write some of the *Songs of Experience* in a cramped and concentrated form, and other drafts and poems almost fill it completely. It appears likely that the *Experience* poems in the manuscript could be assigned to the years 1791–2, but the only poem which can be safely given a later date is *Tirzah*, which was written about 1800.

The reader of *Songs of Innocence and Experience* will realize that many of the poems fall naturally into pairs, with 'contraries' or antitheses, the most obvious example being that of *The Lamb* and *The Tyger*; we must, however, always remember that although the series is seen as an entire concept or two facets of a concept, each poem must stand on its own regardless of the overall impact of the group. The most obvious way of approaching the *Songs* is to read them through quickly and get a general impression of the degrees of 'innocence' or 'experience', thus grasping the essential comparisons and contrasts inherent in their structure. The individual poems can then be looked at in depth and related to the pattern of the whole. Blake uses, for example, the two poems named above to give different pictures of the Divinity – the good God on the one hand and the unfathomable God of fear on the other. Each poem is so strongly individualistic that each tends to support the theory that Blake was outside the 'innocence' and 'experience' which he projects.

But perhaps it should be indicated here what the *Songs* often or commonly possess; for the most part, and this applies particularly to *Innocence*, they are understood on a certain level at once, being attractive to both the eye and the ear. Yet at the same time they have extensions and associations of meaning, certain extra dimensions of which Blake himself may well have been unaware at the time. As Auden wrote of Yeats after his death, 'The words of a dead man/Are modified in the guts of the living', and this admirably defines the complexities of Blake too, whether their making was conscious or unconscious at the time either of writing or of revision. The *Songs* are free from the literary affectations of 18th-century poetry; the intensive personification used by Blake, for example, is part of his own mode of emphasis and not the reflex of convention.

Because of the duality of the conception, there is no heavy-handed moralizing; for the most part there is a fine power in the lyrics, almost as if they are not merely songs but little, exquisite pictures or visions, as indeed they are. The form fits the expression, and is varied and adjusted in *Experience* to make the nature of the retrospective reference clear: as Blake observed, 'Without contraries is no progression'. In view of the weighted associations, the uniqueness of the poetic pendulum, it is interesting to note that in his own lifetime Blake enjoyed scant reputation as a poet. Taken as pairs or opposites, the *Songs* show the dialectic manner of Blake's thought, the two sides of a critical enquiry into the 'state' of man under investigation. We should also note that each of the *Songs* stands up on its own, and that they are enjoyable and stimulating despite the esoteric nature of their complexities, for such directness carries its own appeal. One of Blake's contemporaries said of him that he was 'the most sublime in his expressions, with the simplicity and gentleness of a child', and this must be set against Blake's own assertion that 'Attraction and Repulsion, Reason and Energy, Love and Hate, are necessary to Human Existence'.

Critics and readers over the years have found this marriage of complexity and simplicity, of the interaction of opposites, a stimulating and moving one. Thus Swinburne found in *The Little Black Boy* evidence that 'the poet's mysticism is baptized with pure water', while Allan Cunningham noted the individual quality of the engravings:

Every scene has its poetical accompaniment, curiously interwoven with the group or the landscape, and forming, from the beauty of the colour and prettiness of the pencilling, a very fair picture of itself. These designs are in general highly poetical; more allied, however, to heaven than to earth – a kind of spiritual abstraction, and indicating a better world and fuller happiness than mortals enjoy

While we may not agree with the tone of much of this, the 'more allied, however, to heaven than to earth' does define not only the illustrations but also the profoundly visionary quality of so many of the *Songs*.

The care with which Blake put the poems together, his revisions, and the omissions of certain verses which could well have been included in the complete volume, show a mature artistic awareness as well as the high value he placed upon their quality and their relationship. He adapted the traditional metres of hymn tunes to his needs, and although he was writing his prophetic books at the same time, the *Songs* are quite independent of them. The mythology, the symbolism, is for the most part sufficiently clear-cut and obvious, and they are so lilting that we are charmed and do not, until subsequent readings, see the complexity beneath the translucent surface. C. M. Bowra has put admirably, succinctly, what it is that Blake achieves:

The first part sets out an imaginative vision of the state of innocence: the second shows how life challenges and corrupts and destroys it.

He follows this by quoting the motto to the *Songs of Innocence and Experience*, and this is important to our understanding of the main theme:

> The Good are attracted by Men's perceptions,
> And think not for themselves;
> Till Experience teaches them to catch
> And to cage the Fairies and Elves.
>
> And then the Knave begins to snarl
> And the Hypocrite to howl,
> And all his good Friends show their private ends,
> And the Eagle is known from the Owl.

Some critics have tried to find a reason in Blake's own life for the essential difference between the *Songs of Innocence* and those of *Experience*, and there are those who see the poet as having passed through both a personal and a spiritual crisis. He may indeed have been influenced by the course of the French Revolution, for the ideals of the beginning became the lost illusion of the succeeding years. Whatever the reason, the additional layers of *Experience* are sombre ones, with the simple form overlaid, so to speak, by a weight of symbol. Throughout, many of the symbols, as always in Blake, are Biblical in origin (like the Lamb or the Shepherd), but in *Experience* the private language (as in *The Clod & the Pebble*) reflects the development not merely of evil but of complexity in nature once the days of childhood are passed. Throughout the *Songs* we are aware of one major facet of the duality, the strong sense of compassion and at the other extreme a sense of bitterness at the thrusting out of love.

By the time we come to *London* there is a fearful exposure through a realism which sees things as they are (though with nightmare intensity of vision) and doesn't hesitate to name them; chimney-sweep, soldier, prostitute, all these are the oppressed, while church and crown, representations of the establishment, are the recipients of the poet's wrath. In these *Songs* Blake uses what some have called satire; it seems to this writer that the more correct term is irony, and the measure of his achievement is that he finds a lyrical form consonant with this bitter mood, with each poem so fashioned that it is capable of yielding secondary meanings which are independent of the primary interpretation. Thus the sunflower of *Ah! Sunflower* is symbolic of earth-bound love which tries to follow the sun but which can never escape from its roots; seen in another way, it is the manifestation of an ideal which can never be realized. By showing the states of corruption and frustration Blake is implying that they in turn will be overcome by great power, the wrath of an angry God. Perhaps a unity, too, is hinted at, as in *The Tyger*, where the power in the 'forests of the night' represents a life force which may conquer and compel corruption by its sheer strength. As Bowra puts it explicitly, 'When the Lamb is destroyed by experience, the tiger is needed to restore the world'. This release of creative energy in its visionary form is the hallmark of the *Songs of Experience*.

Summaries of and commentaries on poems, textual notes and revision questions*

Songs of Innocence

Introduction

This poem is made up of five verses of four lines each, with alternate lines rhyming for the most part, though with unrhymed first and third lines in three of the verses. The form is that of the ballad, a song in itself, and the language is simple and repetitive as befits happy and innocent situations. Notice that the key *is* happiness, the number of synonyms for this achieving a cumulative effect ('glee', 'laughing', 'merry chear'), and the movement through the verses is of recurring repetition ('piping', 'pipe', 'piped', 'piper'), with 'And I' marking the final phrase, when the celebration is recorded for all time in the form of a book. Since innocence is equated with simplicity and particularly with childhood, the child on the cloud symbolizes happiness and is obviously to be identified with Christ.

All Blake's poems, however simple their external form, carry symbolic or allegorical overtones, so that this poem is at once a simple celebration of both childhood and Christianity. The technique of using dialogue within the short narration is a commonplace in the ballad form, and is much used by Blake in these songs. The 18th-century convention of heavy personification is absent (the capital in *L*amb gives it recognizable religious associations) and in fact the poem is free from the artificial diction common to the period before the publication of the *Lyrical Ballads* (1798) of Wordsworth and Coleridge. The pastoral elements – the piper, the valleys, the streams – are given an explicitly Christian association as distinct from the pagan

* *Note:* Blake moved some of the Songs from Innocence to Experience. The Little Girl Lost, The Little Girl Found, The School Boy and The Voice of the Ancient Bard are here included in Songs of Experience.

connections usual in poetry – for instance, the pagan piper Pan, the Greek rural deity.

On a cloud Note the visual quality; the cloud here is one of happiness and not, as is more common, of misery. The illustration – and wherever possible these poems should be read with the accompanying engravings – is on a single page before the poem, and shows the cherubic child, with sheep feeding below the cloud which extends lightly between the trees.

he wept to hear Obviously with joy, as in the following verse.

a rural pen i.e. to write of simple country scenes as symbolic of innocence.

I stain'd the water clear The idea is of perpetuating the 'songs' by recording them for others to 'hear'; the reference is to the written word *and* to the accompanying use of water-colours in the engraving. The words and their representation thus focus on the duality of the expression.

A Dream

This beautiful poem is again in five verses, though here each one contains two rhyming couplets. There is, how-ever, a variation: two of the verses have consonant rhymes but not vowel rhymes in one of the couplets, 'shade', 'bed' in verse one and 'hum', 'home' in verse five. Almost cer-tainly derived from one of Isaac Watts's *Divine and Moral Songs for Children*, here the dream is a simple, imaginative exposition; the most insignificant of God's creatures have the capacity to experience suffering but they too can be led to safety by compassion – in this case by the glow-worm's light. The emmet symbolizes both mother-love and the frustrations of life which sever the mother from the young, the need to love and to care for the children being the primary concern. The essential simplicity, the voicing of pain, therefore represents adversity, the specific reference here being almost lost in the universality of the application. The personification, the love of family, is again expressed through the form of monologue which shades into dialogue; it is effectively done because the love expressed is the love of humanity. Perhaps the glow-worm symbolizes the light of heaven, of essential goodness, with the beetle the natural cycle reflecting permanence and thus happiness. The moral theme is that we exist to help others, but the tone throughout is imbued with compassion and tenderness. It is, fittingly, child-like.

weave a shade i.e. depressed (me).
Emmet An ant.
'wildered Bewildered.
benighted Overtaken by night or darkness.
tangled spray i.e. of blossom.
O my children! Note the immediate humanitarian, pitying invocation.
wailing wight Weeping person. The alliteration almost conveys the misery.
the watchman of the night Himself, the glow-worm.
hie thee Take yourself, get.

The Lamb

The beautiful engraving which forms the surround to this poem illustrates the refrain which begins and ends each of the two verses. A child is seen feeding a flock of sheep; this obviously symbolizes love, the kinship of man and nature in a state of innocence. The poem is written as the questioning song of a child, but clearly derives from the perpetual questions we ask ourselves about our origins, from whence creation and all living things come. The Lamb is, of course, once again to be equated with Jesus. The first verse is completely rural in emphasis, the second strongly spiritual, with the linking of the lamb in nature and in God. Because of the use of a refrain this is even more of a song, and the vowel sounds have the softness and repetition both of the bleating of the lamb and of the child lisping the song. The first verse is in the form of a question and the second is in the shape of an answer which reveals the child's certainty in his faith and his innocent acceptance of all its teachings. The repetition of fact and description reflects the simplicity of the conception, and the hymn-like quality is finely sustained. The fact that the child answers for the lamb, which exists in its own inarticulate completeness, gives the poem a moving, tremulous quality.

clothing of delight Because the wool is beautiful and beautiful clothes are made from it.

clothing ... clothing ... called ... calls Note how the repetition, common in Blake *within* the lines, contributes to the music of the verse. It is part of the running alliteration (voice ... vales).

He is called i.e. Christ.

meek ... mild A favourite alliterative usage of Blake's, and the two words most associated with Jesus and the Virgin Mary.

called by his name i.e. in the sense that the child who is 'Christian' is called after Christ.

The Blossom

This is deceptively simple in form, but correspondingly complex and ambiguous in associations. The short six-lined verses have three rhyming lines, then two, then one odd line, though in the second verse the word 'Robin' is repeated as a rhyme. It exists, as great poetry so often does, on a number of levels, but its symbolic overtones are intensely lyrical and seem to indicate that this is more than a mere lullaby. It has been suggested that this is a love poem imbued with passion and movement, almost as if Blake's unconscious or subconscious has been responsible for those additional dimensions of suggestion which are so original and intense in their verbal power, even, one is tempted to suggest, in the innocence of their verbal power. Sparrows are traditionally associated with happiness, and robins occasionally with sadness. Note the regularity *and* the variations, the change of mood conveyed by the use of

'Merry' as distinct from 'Pretty', and the economical nature of both the imagery 'swift as arrow' and the description.

your cradle narrow i.e. the nest.

The Ecchoing Green

This is a poem evocative of children playing in delight and innocence. It consists of three ten-lined verses written in rhyming couplets depicting the natural cycle of life from dawn in the first verse 'The Sun does arise' to dusk in the third verse 'The sun does descend'. The second stanza represents the middle years with the old folk looking back on their own youth when they too 'were seen/On the ecchoing green'. The third verse forms a fine contrast, capturing for all time the inevitability of change, with the children having left the 'darkening green' and going home 'to the laps of their mothers'. The imagery is simple and reflects the unity of man and nature 'Like birds in their nest'. The unity of the life cycle, the links and the natural continuity between old and young, the enduring ties of habit and of love, though seen idealistically, are none the less moving and complete. Love is the key, but it is the love with which Blake imbues the poem, the love for pleasures which transcend the present and are for all time – of the simple things, birds, bells, the old and young in memory and freedom.

The Ecchoing Green The village green or field where the children shout in their play and the birds sing – hence the echoes.
laugh away care Old John finds peace in the laughter of children.
Like birds in their nest Though the simile is a simple one, it is fundamental to our appreciation of the poem. It represents the care and love of family life (and its security) in nature and in man – and the essential innocence of both.

The Divine Image

A rare perfection of form is attained in this poem, by the
rhythmic flow and counter-flow of the four personifications
which constitute the sublime content of these verses. They
are called 'virtues of delight' by Blake, and the poem
praises both God, in whom they all exist, and man, the
image of God. Blake held that the true attributes of man are
those of Christ, and the divine attributes of Christ are those
of 'the true Man' (*All Religions Are One*). This assertion of
the identification of God with man, and of man with God, is
the core of the poem and of Blake's belief and faith at the
time. The influence is undoubtedly that of the mystical
Emmanuel Swedenborg (1688–1772), who, after a long
study of science, suddenly switched his serious attentions to
theology, living a simple life thereafter, and believing that
the only real world was the spirit-world. The Sweden-
borgians founded a church based on his teaching, which
saw God as incarnate in the divine humanity of Christ. The
first two verses are balanced by the invocation, the second
linking God and man in a divine relationship, that of father
and child. The poem marks a return to the ballad form,
with the personifications and gentle, lilting repetitions and
reinvocations carrying it along; the repetitions are very
significant, for in the third and fourth verses the word
'human' occurs five times, indicative, perhaps, of the
humanity which informs the poem. It traces a circle of love
and reason which brings all the 'virtues of delight' back to
man, who is the image of God.

Mercy, Pity, Peace, and Love Note the choice in a kind of
  ascending worth – God is Love.
And Peace, the human dress i.e. the outwardness of man,
  living in harmony with others.
clime Country.
And all must love the human form The universality of love
  which transcends the narrowness of any sect is what Blake is
  indicating here.

The Chimney Sweeper

This poem written in rhyming couplets has six verses of four lines each. Though the poem is simple and visionary on one level, contrasting the misery of life with the joy of visionary experience – here seen to sustain the young Sweep through the hardships of the coming day – the comment in the last line, deliberate or otherwise, under-lines the puritanical idea of duty in no uncertain terms. The irony is quite apparent, too, in the use of the now familiar image of the lamb, perhaps without capitals here to indi-cate the reduction of man by man. In fact the innuendo and the symbolic overtones give this poem a greater density than those we have seen hitherto, as the textual notes below will indicate.

my father sold me The price was roughly between 2 guineas and 8 guineas.

'weep, weep, weep' Notice that the sound captures at once the monotony of crying and the 'cheep' sound of a bird, the irony being that the boy's 'nest' (and 'coffin') is the chimney.

I sweep Notice the internal rhyme which adds to the plaintive quality of the song.

curl'd like a lamb's back There is unobtrusive natural observation in this image, but note that the lamb is *not* the Lamb of God in this context, a sufficient commentary on man's inhumanity to man. The children's heads were shaved so that their hair would not flame up from the burning soot sometimes to be found in the chimneys.

white hair Indicative of beauty and innocence, compared with the blackness of the soot *and* of the heart of man which is responsible for this evil practice.

he had such a sight i.e. a dream or vision.

lock'd up in coffins of black A fine symbolic representation of the chimney and of the early death which befell so many children by suffocation.

their bags In which they carried chimney brushes and, perhaps, in which they stored soot.

They rise ... sport in the wind The image is classical in origin, but here because of the boys' deprivation it is strongly, effectively visual.

And the Angel told Tom The angel, though protective, and implying that this life is a preparation for the next, sufficiently indicates the suffering of the children.

God for his father An ironic contrast, a reference back to his real father. The emphasis here is on love.

never want joy Never *lack* joy.

we rose in the dark Of the morning, when boy sweeps set out to work. Their hours were supposedly limited by an act of 1788, which also established that they had to be eight years old before being employed. Naturally, hours and age were both abused, a damning indictment of the times.

So if all do ... harm Clearly by 'duty' Blake does not mean 'assigned task' but the duty of all men, e.g. our duty to Tom. There is the sting of our own failure in this statement.

Infant Joy

This poem consists of two six-lined verses, of very short lines and a supposed dialogue and a refrain. The contemplation of the baby invokes a mood of ecstatic acceptance and blessing for the miracle of birth and the state of innocence. The song is simplicity itself, 'Joy' being the name applicable to the child in its state of joy rather than its baptismal name. The word is the key to the poem, the lyrical celebration without adornment or pretentiousness, a prayer for that state to continue throughout its life.

I happy am Note the inversion of the word order to convey the 'joy' or happiness.

Sweet joy befall thee May you be happy in life.

The Shepherd

Two rhythmically conventional verses, quatrains, which glorify the shepherd in his simple way of life and, by Biblical association, equate the shepherd symbolically with God (remember the 23rd psalm, for example, 'The Lord is my

shepherd, I shall not want'). This is simple spiritual exposition, without dialogue, unflawed by comment or
decoration.

their Shepherd is nigh Their God is near.

Night

Six eight-lined verses, cleverly varied by having the first
four lines in each rhyming alternately, with the last four in
rhyming couplets. The language is very simple, and the
mood expresses the relationship between God and nature.
Thus the first verse contemplates the heavens at night, then
turns to man and nature seeking rest. The second verse
further connects the animal kingdom with the kingdom of
God, for angels watch over all that is in nature from sheep
to flowers. The third verse conveys the extent and range of
that watching, with an abiding concern for peace and tranquillity in sleep. The fourth verse marks a transition, with
the animals of prey sometimes succeeding in snatching
their victims and the angels receiving the souls of the
slaughtered innocents in heaven. This leads into the final
two verses, the theme of which is reconciliation in the
afterlife, with the lion lying down with the lamb, and indeed the beasts of prey protecting the innocent. The poem
is obviously allegorical, the lambs and the lions representing innocence and strength, the existence of the 'contraries'
in man. Again it is an expression, visionary in form as one
sees from the illustrations, of an abiding faith.

like a flower Fine simple image – as night progresses, so the
 moon 'opens'.
Sits and smiles on the night So strongly is the poet
 identifying with nature and the night that this personification
 almost goes unnoticed.
took delight ... silent moves 'took' would be acceptable for
 'taken' in 18th-century English (in fact it would be the current
 usage), but 'moves' should be 'move' to agree with 'feet'.

blessing ... ceasing ... blossom ... bosom Notice how
  Blake re-works earlier rhymes and subjects with ease into this
  verse.
thoughtless nest All is natural, not thinking, just acting by
  instinct. This is the best part of innocence.
pour sleep The idea is 'from above', i.e. heaven.
pitying stand and weep This implies divine compassion for
  suffering.
their thirst i.e. for blood.
they rush dreadful i.e. the wolves and tygers.
New worlds to inherit i.e. the afterlife, in heaven.
Wrath ... meekness ... health ... sickness A fine use of
  'contraries' to indicate the triumph of God – Love – on earth,
  and, here, in 'our immortal day', the life everlasting.
And now beside thee, bleating lamb ... The reference is to
  Isaiah, 11,6: 'The wolf shall dwell with the lamb, and the
  leopard shall lie down with the kid; and the calf and the lion
  and the fatling together; and a little child shall lead them.'
wash'd in life's river Presumably cleansed through the
  experience of life. 'Life's river' is also part of the landscape of
  Heaven in Revelation, 22,1.

A Cradle Song

The influence is *A Cradle Hymn*, by Isaac Watts, and the
skill of the poem lies in the beautiful weaving of the vowel
sounds and the repetitions; they have a musical lilt and do
not cloy, so insistent is the rhythm and the purity of diction
and sentiment. Each four-lined verse consists of two rhyming couplets, with one rhyme – smiles, beguiles – repeated
three times. The alliteration is almost like a child's lisp
in terms of its contributory musical quality. The internal
rhymes are reinforced (note particularly the 'i' sounds), the
consonant sounds are finely echoed, and the repeated posi-
tioning of certain words (six of the eight verses begin with
the word 'sleep') helps to establish the loving mood. The
emphasis is certainly on love again, but this is a 'song' in
the true sense of the word, since its music is felt by the ear
and seen by the eye whether we read it silently or aloud.

form a shade i.e. protection.

Be happy, silent, moony beams Notice the way in which the single words are suggestive of sleep, tranquil rest.

soft down i.e. bird's underplumage used to stuff eiderdowns, and so typifying sleep.

beguiles Charms during sleep.

dovelike signs i.e. very light – the dove has long been associated with innocence.

thy mother weep i.e. with happiness at the contemplation of innocence.

Holy image i.e. the infant Jesus.

wept for me Notice how the line here is run on in repetition, breaking completely with the 18th-century tradition of self-contained verses.

Thou his image ever see May you always be conscious of the influence of Jesus (and thus of God).

to peace beguiles i.e. the reconciliation through the love of God.

The Little Boy Lost

Two simple verses, the first in the plaintive voice of the child, the second a description of being lost. The use of dialogue dear to Blake is again used in this short ballad form, while the simplicity of the child's speech might be compared with one of Wordsworth's rural ballads. The sudden switch from dialogue is very effective, since the repetitive 'The' with which three lines of this verse begin, shows the extent of the isolation and loneliness.

And away the vapour flew This has to be read in conjunction with the poem which follows it here (*The Little Boy Found*), where the 'wand'ring light' is referred to. It seems that the child has been misled by a will-o'-the-wisp and that only God can save him.

The Little Boy Found

The form is as in the previous poem, the internal rhyme occurring in the third line of each of the verses. God presents himself before the child dressed in white symbolic of faith and innocence.

the wand'ring light See note on the previous poem.
by the hand led Note the omission of 'him' in the interests of economy.

Nurse's Song

The poem indicates, in the same way as in *The Ecchoing Green*, the happiness and innocence enjoyed by all those who watch children at play. Again the form is the quatrain, with an internal rhyme in the third line of each verse, though admittedly by the fourth verse consonance has replaced pure rhyme. The first verse is redolent of tranquillity, for the nurse can hear the children's voices; this gives way in the second verse to a plea to the children to come in – again note the use of dialogue – while the third verse contains the children's answer, a plea to play on and on, just as the birds are still flying and the hills have sheep on them. The fourth contains the nurse's reply, the injunction to continue their play until it is time to 'go home to bed'. The children play on, and 'all the hills echoed', which further indicates that the theme of the poem is innocent happiness. Once again the familiar symbols of that innocence – children, birds, sheep – are used, while the rhythmic movement of the verse somehow harmonizes with the movement of the children playing.

Holy Thursday

This beautiful poem, written in rhyming couplets and in much longer lines, subtly captures by this increased length the sense of a procession of children. Blake is referring here to the Charity Schools' services at St Paul's Cathedral on Ascension Day, when the average attendance numbered between four and five thousand. Just as the Thames forms an important part of Blake's Song of Experience called

London, so here the onward flow of the children in faith and innocence is paralleled to the flow of the mighty river. The beauty of the second verse lies in the fact that the children are multitudes of flowers, lambs, which of course recalls Christ feeding the multitude of 5000 with the fish and loaves (Matthew, 14,15–21). Here these children are fed, if you like, with the miracle of faith. In the third verse, the children invoke heaven in their songs of praise, and Blake counsels the reader to be full of compassion for the poor, 'lest you drive an angel from your door'. The lines are also resonant with the sound of voices, the songs and hymns of praise.

Holy Thursday Ascension Day, the celebration on the 40th day after the Resurrection.

beadles Ceremonial officers, perhaps here representing the companies that endowed the schools, or perhaps Parish officers.

wands as white as snow A brief simile symbolic of innocence.

of Paul's i.e. St Paul's Cathedral.

Thames' waters Remember that the Thames would be the focus of London life at this time.

in companies i.e. each within their separate school groups. Blake is also paralleling another gathering of the multitude: 'And he commanded them to make all sit down by companies' (Mark, 6,39).

the seats of heaven among Note the inverted word order, a common device in Blake, and used for emphasis.

aged men i.e. the beadles.

On Another's Sorrow

This poem marks a return to the shorter lines, each verse being in rhyming couplets and having four lines. The first two verses are given over entirely to the suffering of others and our identification with it. This theme is emphasized in the third verse by making the sufferer a child and asserting that a fullness of sympathetic 'giving' is the lot of the mother. The next three verses transfer the loving identification to God's care for all in nature and humanity, with the implication running throughout that man, in God's image, exerts the same care, a care for all who suffer in innocence. Once again birds and children are symbolic of that innocence. The final three verses express ecstatically the identification of the creator with all that he has created, the allegory of the poem asserting that God is with us whenever he is needed, that he is the sharer of all our woes and thus our comforter. The technique of question and repeated answer is equivalent to dialogue; the language is, as always, simple, with the usual alliterative and lyrical flair, the fineness of the sympathy moving from the human to the divine plane, from the family to the natural to the universal love and care of God, seen in his identification with man through the infant Christ. The extraordinary quality of this poem, with its question and answer techniques, is attributable to the fact that the poet does not use a single image with which to embroider the simple expression of his faith and his love of God.

my sorrow's share i.e. the grief I feel at the tears of another.
he who smiles on all i.e. God.
Hear the wren Note the repetition of these lines – God's concern is 'repeated' for all.
sit the cradle near Inverted word order for the sake of the rhyme.
He doth give ... Again the repetition, with the same effect as previously noted.
He becomes and infant small i.e. Jesus.
a man of woe Christ at the Crucifixion.
And thy maker The repetition underlines the universality of God.
sit by us and moan i.e. grieves with us.

Spring

Three very simple verses, a salute to the New Year in three-syllabled lines capped in each case by the longer, ringing refrain. Man's instrument (the flute) precedes the voices of the birds in the first verse (though all are indicative of universal harmony). In the second children are linked with the cock crowing, while the third verse is entirely to do with the lamb, an obvious symbol for the infant Jesus; the child-like caresses stress the nature of innocent faith and accept-ance. There is a sure lyrical touch throughout, and the fine vowel sounds are part of the music of this charming song.

it's mute i.e. silent.
Little Girl Hardly a rhyme for 'small' unless pronounced 'gal' – and this is probably how Blake said it.

Laughing Song

Here again the four-lined verse is employed but this time with rhyming couplets. It is indeed a laughing song, the longer lines stressing the delight in nature and the harmony between man and nature; there is an easy personification of the woods, the streams, the meadows even down to the smallness of the grasshopper. The voices of the girls conjure an idyllic scene and Blake's use of simple language, with clear, clean vowel sounds reflects both harmony and joy. The fourth verse, with its echoes of Shakespeare and, cer-tainly, Marlowe ('Come live with me and be my love') has a fine natural refrain. The alliterative qualities stem largely from the light 'l' sounds and repetition, as always, is marked.

dimpling Finely observant word to indicate the ripples.
the painted birds Note this description – meaning painted by the hand of nature, or of God.

The Little Black Boy

Here there are seven four-lined verses, built on contrast and imbued with love and compassion of a singular kind, with an enlightenment and vision which transcends race –

in other words, this is a poem well before its time. Again the
vowel sounds are marked, the quatrains having alternate
lines rhyming, with a clear pattern of associated light and
dark imagery. The key, as always in these songs, is love,
natural, unforced, one might say superbly unselfconscious.
The white/black contrast is evident from the first verse,
spoken by the African child, with the ominous word 'bereav'd' showing the poet's awareness of the earthly category
of difference. His mother explains how God abiding in the
East gives comfort and strength to all his creatures and that
his black face is only a temporary cloud. Earthly life, with
the abiding goodness of God, is shown to be but a preparation for the spiritual hereafter. In the final two verses, the
Black Boy explains to the English child that they are both
equals and that neither can be free until they depart from
the physical world. He even suggests that when they gather
in 'the tent of God' his black skin will shield the English
boy until he too can bear God's beams of Love. The concept of the black and white clouds is a mystical one, but the
idea of universal love – white, black, God-encompassing –
impregnates this fine poem.

southern wild i.e. Africa. Blake's father belonged to a
  religious sect which was greatly concerned with missionary
  work.
white ... black The central contrast – and unity – of the
  poem.
bereav'd Fine choice of word, here meaning 'as if dead' (to
  spiritual whiteness).
And flowers and trees Again the linking of God and nature.
Is but a cloud i.e. covering us – not showing our spirits.
learn'd the heat to bear i.e. learned to accept *and* to return
  the love of God.
his silver hair Blake writes often in simple colours, as here.
And be like him ... Some critics have seen a sense of
  complacency or a patronizing tone here – but this is to
  misunderstand Blake, whose important emphasis is as always
  the universality of love.

Revision Questions on Songs of Innocence

1 By close reference to two or three poems, indicate Blake's use of the ballad form.

2 What part does *dialogue* play in these poems? You should refer to at least three or four poems in your answer.

3 Examine Blake's presentation of his themes in two or three of these songs.

4 In what ways are these poems either visual or visionary?

5 Write an essay on Blake's favourite images of innocence. In what ways are the poems themselves 'innocent'?
(Remember that these poems are called 'Songs'. Why do you think Blake called them 'Songs'? You might think about song for its sound, or for its subject, or for its harmonizing of the two. Make a list of qualities which you think a song should have (for example, rhyme, rhythm, a clear theme) and then pick out, say, three of Blake's poems and see whether they conform to your definition of a song – a definition which you compare with the one in the dictionary. Now look closely again at Blake's 'Songs' and see whether there are any which do not fit the definition. If you find any, say why, by quotation and reference, you think they do not fit.)

Songs of Experience

Introduction

This is naturally the first poem in the sequence, and is always followed by *Earth's Answer*. Both poems are written in exactly the same form, that is with the first, third and fourth lines rhyming together, then the second and fifth. Once again dialogue is used, as indeed it is in *Earth's Answer*. The contrast with the introductory poem of the *Innocence* sequence is obvious, and perhaps it should be said here that *all* the poems should be read as pairs or 'contraries', with 'innocence' as the ideal and 'experience' as a kind of visionary reality. Here the piper of innocence has been replaced by the all-seeing Bard of experience. Innocence required simplicity and clarity, whereas experience almost invites obscurity; thus the first verse urges the reader to note what the prophet-poet says in the ensuing poems, for he sees everything, right back to the Fall of Man in the Garden of Eden, 'The Holy Word/That walked among the ancient trees'. The second verse appears to be a plea for the 'lapsed soul' (whether Satan or mankind or both), asking those in the fallen state to renew their faith in God. In the next two verses Blake appears to suggest that such a return or renewal will herald a new era of faith on earth; hence, 'Earth' should not reject it.

Bard Poet.
Present, Past, & Future The capitals show us how far away from innocence we are, since these reflect the gamut of experience.
The Holy Word A reference to Genesis, 3,8: 'And they heard the voice of the Lord God walking in the garden.'
the ancient trees Adam and Eve hid themselves among the trees after their transgression in the Garden of Eden.
the lapsed Soul i.e. those fallen, perhaps personified by Satan

(Lucifer fell from heaven – he was the brightest of the angels hitherto).

the starry pole i.e. the heavens.

Night ... The wat'ry shore Darkness and insecurity, uncertainty, symbols of a lack of faith.

morn ... break of day A new era, of faith.

till i.e. only till day – the new era referred to above – arrives.

Earth's Answer

Written in the same form as the previous poem, which Earth in her answer parodies. The personification in the first verse is overlaid with despair and misery, almost Miltonic in tone and in visual association, and the following four verses convey Earth's bitterness and lack of faith: she is not consoled by being given the 'starry floor' or the 'wat'ry shore'. Two of these four verses end with unanswered questions and underline the nature of the suffering, the rejection of God, who is seen as tyrannical. In the second verse two of the symbols used in the Introduction recur: the 'wat'ry shore' is now a prison and 'Starry Jealousy' – the jealous Creator of the material world – keeps Earth chained below in a 'den'. The last line of this verse leads directly into the next, which stigmatizes God as selfish, and then goes on to elaborate on this theme and the consequent reduction of man. The fourth verse brings us back to nature, using it as a parallel to God's jealousy of man. God does not delight in man as nature delights in what it creates through sowing the seed. Again night is the symbol of agony or unnaturalness. The last verse is more of a plea than an answer, a plea for freedom from the curse of selfishness which is God's doing – 'That free Love with bondage bound'. It has been rightly noted that the odd rhymes in verses three and four, and the rhythmic variations, underline the consonance between the theme and a certain deliberate roughness in the verse. This appropriately underlines the subject matter of the poem. Blake's structures are simple but subtle too, in the sense that what is said and the manner of saying it are perfectly blended.

Earth raised up Heavy personification, which runs throughout the verse. Compare this with Milton's treatment of the fallen angels in the first book of *Paradise Lost*, or Keats's presentation of the overthrown Titans in *Hyperion*.

dread & drear Note the heavy alliteration, running throughout, which reflects the mood.

I hear the father i.e. the Word of God (see *Introduction*, line 4).

Chain'd in night Imprisoned in darkness.

night ... darkness Note that what is being described is unnatural – like the 'selfishness' of God.

chain ... freeze my bones ... bondage bound i.e. man has been imprisoned, enslaved by God. Note the heavy repetitions of the 'prison' imagery.

free Love i.e. freedom to express love – for man, for God.

The Clod & the Pebble

In this poem the Clod of Clay sings the praises of unselfish love (Innocence), while the Pebble exalts selfish love and so symbolizes experience. The Clod of Clay puts the altruistic view – remember that clay is malleable, human – whereas the pebble, lying in the waters of materialism, fittingly puts the opposite view. The dialogue, the balancing of viewpoints, occupies verses one and three, the middle verse defining the imaginary speakers. In the first verse, we see that love renders all things bearable through its selflessness as it exists for others or another alone, and there is a fine antithetical balance in the last line of the first verse. The symbolism of the second verse is particularly interesting: the Clod is experiencing suffering, but the Pebble's voice, perhaps echoing the voice of the water in the brook, speaks in 'metres meet' and goes on to expand the idea that love exists only to please itself, to subjugate others or another to its will, and corrupts where before there was purity. The third verse is thus a deliberate turning about of the first.

You should pay particular attention to the form of this poem, with its precise balancing of 'contraries'.

hath any care i.e. it is outward looking, having no concern for itself.

builds a Heaven in Hell's despair i.e. unselfish love builds a Heaven to the despair of the Hell of selfishness.

Warbled . . . metres meet The first word is sufficiently vague, and the alliteration of the next two conveys the sophistication – experience – of the worldly view.

To bind . . . Its delight i.e. to use for its own gratification.

Joys in another's loss of ease Takes delight in the discomfort of another, of somebody else.

And builds a Hell The reversal of the first verse, here meaning 'makes miserable and corrupt despite being placed in a situation of beauty and happiness'.

Holy Thursday

In a poem of the same name in *Songs of Innocence*, Blake described the parade of charity school children in St Paul's. However, in this poem the children are reduced to victims of social injustice. The four quatrains, short-lined and with alternate lines rhyming, display a clever technique in which there are unanswered questions while at the same time *some* of the questions are answered by the worst kind of affirmative. Here charity is an indictment rather than an act of pity. Verse one makes it clear that what the poor children receive is given unfeelingly and with an eye to the cost; here the song and its burden of joy is viewed ironically in view of the poverty of those singing it. The 'eternal winter', in a verse of natural description meant to parallel the state of the poor children, is the symbol of desolation and suffering, and the last verse continues this theme by saying that 'sun' and 'rain' – the beneficence of nature – keep children alive as distinct from man-made poverty and the squalor of their living conditions. The poem asserts a bitterness based on an underlying realism. Blake is not merely a visionary. He is also socially aware and a powerful critic of physical, moral and spiritual deprivation in his time.

Holy Thursday Ascension Day. See note, p. 29.

usurous hand i.e. calculating (related to usury – the lending of money at inflated interest).

song ... song ... poor ... poverty Part of Blake's effect is achieved by a repetition which is here both ironic and realistic.

And their sun The beginning of a repetitive sequence rather like the verse of a hymn, and, hence, here ironic.

bleak & bare Note the hardness of the alliteration, as befits the subject.

fill'd with thorns Note the Biblical associations with the crown of thorns made for Christ – here the 'torture' of poverty is being stressed.

appall Just as in *London*, there is a half pun (the 'pall' of the coffin) here which carries the symbolic overtone of death.

The Little Girl Lost

Both this poem and *The Little Girl Found* were originally composed by Blake for *Songs of Innocence*. Perhaps this reveals both Blake's inherent self-awareness of intention and his capacity for self-criticism. The lines are much shorter, and the effect is somewhat staccato. Thematically – here child lost, there mother lost – it is linked to *A Dream*, but the length of the poem and its distinctive structure are different. The dialogue of the ballad form is again present, but the movement of the poem is considered and integrated. The first two verses (all are of four lines in rhyming couplets) contain a brief but visionary anticipation of the transformation of the 'wild' into love for the 'maker'. Indeed the story that follows is emblematic of the reconciliation between what is wild and untamed with what is innocent and lost. The next six verses describe the somewhat idyllic wandering of the child Lyca until she is lost, worried, and calls to mind her worrying parents, after which she sleeps. The beasts of prey and the animals gather around her, and eventually carry her off 'To caves', but not before the lion, as king of beasts, has licked her and wept at the contemplation of her innocence. The tone is therefore optimistic, foretelling the linking of nature and man in love; as befits a song or moral story, it is set removed from experience (in an idealized 'southern clime') and thus its allegorical overtone comes across clearly and directly. Again notice the extreme simplicity of form and utterance.

(Grave the sentence deep) A reference to his own art (engraving) and meaning also 'note well what is said or observed'..

maker meek Note the inverted word-order, reminiscent of Milton.

a garden mild Symbolic of innocence (before the Fall, before experience).

Lyca A name probably made up by Blake; the name is sweet-sounding, almost echoing 'lyre' and 'lyric', and is thus consonant with the mood of the poem.

told i.e. counted, numbered.

If her heart does ake Note that the mood of child and parent is in harmony, thus reflecting their love.

frowning ... moon Note the repetition and the contrast in this verse.

beasts of prey This appears ominous until we read on, when the theme becomes Biblical – 'the lion shall lie down with the lamb'.

gambol'd Played (with delight).

hallow'd Sacred, here to the innocence of the 'virgin' child.

Ruby tears Note the superb effect of colour and, indeed, of size.

naked Symbolic of the state of innocence.

The Little Girl Found

This is the sequel to the previous poem, and is complementary in form, though the internal structure is somewhat different. The first five verses deal with the search of the parents and their fantasy nightmares about Lyca. The next three verses describe the encounter with the lion and end with the beast licking their hands; in the last five verses the parents recognize his 'spirit arm'd in gold', and his kingly nature as he leads them to the sleeping child. The last of these five verses is very significant, since it implies the complete reconciliation of man and beast in mutual spirituality and love. The theme is thus the same as that in the previous poem. The rhyming couplets are cleverly varied to fit the mood of the searching parents, but flow with regularity, and, hence, tranquillity, in the final section. Notice how one verse sometimes flows into another, a further instance of Blake's freedom from the constrictions of 18th-century formality, and notice also the running alliteration which contributes to the melody of the verse.

the desarts weep The phrase underlines the identification of man and nature, a kind of sympathetic consonance.

seven days ... seven nights The words approximate to the account of the Creation in the first book of Genesis.

The fancied image i.e. of the child, seen in the dreams, of the parents.

Famish'd Reduced to extreme hunger.

prest Pressed on (though she is soon to stop).

bore/Her A good example of the run-on line which is not tied to poetic convention.

couching Lying with body resting on legs.

allay Put at rest.

A Spirit arm'd in gold A wonderful and sudden raising of the narrative tension – a moment of direct revelation, ennobling and unifying at the same time.

a crown ... golden hair Fine visual transformation of the lion *transformed* in the parents' eyes to something Godlike.

In a lonely dell i.e. a small hollow or valley. (Blake's engraving of this is particularly fine, for it depicts a lion and a lioness at the foot of a tremendous twisted tree, and children playing, talking with them.)

The Chimney Sweeper

No vision alleviates the effect of this poem, and the accompanying illustration emphasizes the pathos and suffering. Notice the depersonalization of the child in the eyes of authority, 'A little black thing', while the dialogue is used to probe the abject conditions. The savagery of the attack, of the callousness and cruelty of authority, is seen in the final verse where 'God and his Priest and King' are all blamed for the state of such children. The width of the indictment takes in not only the establishment but also the parents, who, while exploiting their child, believe they do him no harm as he appears happy. The poem, however, makes it clear that he is happy *in spite of* his 'clothes of death'. There is a vivid contrast between the life of a child should have 'happy upon the heath' and the suffering to which it is reduced by those who 'make up a heaven of our misery'. In fact, this song is a plaintive cry.

'weep, weep' See note on *The Chimney Sweeper* in *Innocence*.
They are both gone up to the church i.e. the Church condoned this cruelty.
the clothes of death i.e. black (stained by soot) and the living death which they are suffering.
notes of woe Note the repetition of the phrase which echoes the perpetual misery of the child.
a heaven of our misery A variant of a 'Heaven in Hell's despair'.

Nurse's Song

Here again Blake parodies the previous song in *Innocence*. Now that the children are older, the Nurse does not hear laughter on the hill but whisperings in the dale and she recalls the days of her youth. In the second verse, she tells how her spring was wasted and warns her charges that their winter will be spoilt by secret longings and disillusions. It is a cynical little poem, but exquisitely balanced in the cycle of nature (sun ... dews ... spring ... winter).

whisp'rings Furtive talk among the lovers.
My face turns green and pale At the thought of unfulfilled experiences.
spring and your day ... winter and night Youth and old age, the first implicitly here a time of waste, the second of concealment.

The Sick Rose

Some critics have seen the rose as corrupt, or perhaps capable of corruption, its outward beauty a snare, while others have seen the poem as fraught with sexual implications, with sex here as the obverse of that expressed in *The Blossom*. The simple fact is that here we are shown nature diseased by the experience of the 'invisible worm' which destroys buds and leaves. The poem stands in no need of further esoteric interpretation, since Blake is describing corruption in nature just as he elsewhere describes corruption in man overtly – and the two obviously reflect and suggest each other.

thy bed/Of crimson This, together with the 'worm', obviously accounts for the sexual suggestions in the poem.
dark secret love Appetite, lust for what it (the worm) is getting.

The Fly

In this poem the verses correspond in shape to the smallness of the fly. Blake compares man and insect in the worlds in which they live, the thoughtless brushing away of the fly by man being comparable to society's treatment of man himself. Again the questions, the first-person speech, all make for poignancy and sharpness of utterance. In the fourth verse, Blake equates man's 'thought' and the joy of a fly; both are manifestations of a divine impulse and are therefore immortal. The fly or the man might die but what is essential to each will remain (thought or joy).

Thy summer's play Note the imaginative projection, which sees one of the smallest of God's creatures as enjoying itself.

thoughtless Notice how this links with the idea of 'thought' later in the poem (a thoughtless action can bring death to the fly) and compare this with the usage in *Night* in *Songs of Innocence*.

Am not I At this stage, Blake is underlining the unity between man and all created things.

blind hand Note the fine transference – this is equivalent to 'thoughtless' above.

The Angel

In some ways this is the counterpart of *A Dream*. The four verses each have four lines, with two rhyming couplets to each verse. The dream of the Maiden Queen represents the contrast between youth and age. In her youth she was guarded by an angel but she simulated grief to attract pity and the angel flew away. In verse three the angel re-appears, but it is altogether too late, for she is too old to enjoy it. Here the stress is on the hindsight which experience brings, but the loss is great, for youth has fled. Notice the question at the beginning, and you will realize that this is an interpretation of a dream.

Witless woe was ne'er beguiled! i.e. thoughtless grief was never charmed (by the presence of the angel).

my heart's delight My secret love.

with ten thousand shields and spears She is now irredeemably lost.

For the time of youth was fled Innocence had permanently gone.

The Tyger

The most celebrated of Blake's songs, frequently included in anthologies, with the tiger representing natural power and God seen as the maker of such agents of destruction who have, as the expression of their perfection or symmetry, a tremendous completeness of nature. The poem consists entirely of unanswered questions, but its central image sees God as the divine blacksmith creating from the forge of primitive energy (this was Blake's favourite image for artistic creation). The six verses of four lines each are in rhyming couplets, with fine 'i' sounds and an insistent rhythmic beat, the kind of pounding rhythm which the poet sees as the 'framing' accompanying the tiger; it also conveys the movement of the beast. Thus the symbol of strength, of beauty, and of destruction is enclosed in a symmetry of form, with the first verse having the word 'could' – the ability of the divine creator to fashion such a beast – which in the final verse becomes 'dare' – a mixture of wonder and terror at the achievement of such power which touches on religious awe. The abbreviated, staccato phrases of the third and fourth verses seem to reflect the savage movements of what is savage, but the accompanying descriptions are vivid in both their sound and sense effects. The whole, as so often in Blake, is a painting as well as a poem, from the superb invocation of the opening to the tremendous power of the ending. The tiger is supposedly the Tyger of Wrath, and its might stands in contradistinction to the lambs which fill the verses and illustrations of innocence.

burning bright i.e. the colour, the eyes, the 'glow' of powerful energy.

forests of the night Note the nightmare power of association and fear in this symbol. The tiger is a beast of prey.

Could frame Was able to make.

On what wings ... What the hand 'What' is one of the key words in the poem, implying here the extraordinary nature of the creator.

twist the sinews of thy heart i.e. have the power to fashion and fit them into place.

What the hammer? The creation of the tiger is seen as an act of craftsmanship in a divine forge – but note that the power and the noise are echoes of the Industrial Revolution.

dread grasp i.e. dreadful or dreaded hold (note the repetition of 'dread').

When the stars threw down their spears These symbolize the angels – the fallen angels defeated by God and thus surrendering to him. There is an inevitable reminiscence of *Paradise Lost*.

Did he smile God smiled the smile of the artist who has created a world which contains both lamb and tiger, good and evil, etc.

Dare frame Emphasizes the daring inherent in a creation which combines both beauty and terror.

My Pretty Rose Tree

Two quatrains with alternate lines rhyming, which reflect a situation which might have occurred between Blake and his wife or any other married couple: the man is offered the chance of an extramarital affair but turns it down, as he is faithful to his wife. However, on returning to his wife, he is met only with reproaches. Blake appears to satirize not only female irrationality but also the man's acceptance and adherence to conventional morality: he is suggesting that to react to what is natural (instinct) is to court unhappiness.

Ah! Sun-Flower

Again the linking of nature and man, with the sunflower symbolizing man's aspirations. Youth and the Virgin 'shrouded in snow' indicate the frustrations of earthly, sexual desire, which can only reach fulfilment in heaven. There are two quatrains which have alternate lines rhyming, but with simple and effective contrasting imagery of heat and cold.

countest the steps of the Sun i.e. as it rises.

pined away with desire Grown thin with frustration.

shrouded in snow i.e. sexual frigidity or repression, here to be equated with a kind of death.

The Lilly

A simple four-line verse in which the 'Lilly', a symbol of innocent love, is contrasted with the mock modesty of the rose and the cowardly sheep that feigns bravery. The 'Lilly' is therefore the symbol of purity, as it makes no attempt to pretend to be what it is not.

The Garden of Love

A brilliantly ironic, bitter poem confronting natural innocence with repression. Once again this is in quatrains with alternate lines rhyming, but with a variant in the last verse, where the absence of rhyme strikes the exact note of discord which echoes the bitterness of the poet. The title is itself ironic, measuring the change from the innocence of child play 'Where I used to play on the green' to the 'Thou shalt not', indicating the negative approach of repressive religious institutions. The idea of flowers being replaced by graves and tombstones symbolizes the death of the spirit as well as the natural death which comes with the passage of time (remember the traditional poem 'Where are all the flowers gone?'). The priests, who should be God's agents of love, are the effective repressors of its expression.

A Chapel Symbolic of the Church, perhaps even of a sect; certainly to be equated with authority in religion.
'Thou shalt not' Effectively the reference is to the Ten Commandments – prohibition here rather than the freedom of expression.
sweet flowers i.e. symbols of innocence and love.
And binding with briars A reference to the crown of thorns. See note, p. 38.

The Little Vagabond

Four verses again rich in irony, with rhyming couplets except in the opening lines of verse one. The picture presented is one characteristic of the London poor right through to the time of Dickens and beyond. Blake boldly faces the social and spiritual issues by asking whether children would be better if the church provided what the ale-house now provides – warmth, drink. The theme of the first part is that the denial of comfort leads only to suffering, in the afterlife as well, while the second indicates what the church could provide; the third asserts a framework for the coming together in prayer and goodness and genuine Christianity (perhaps changing the suffering of individuals for instance). The Vagabond's *naïveté* and pure heart have transformed the Parson and dame Lurch into charitable figures and he clearly sees God as a loving, not a threatening, father.

Dear Mother The phrase carries its own irony for the forsaken child.

Such usage in heaven will never do well Note the repetition of 'well' and the fact that heaven is to be equated with comfort and warmth.

our souls to regale Somewhat clumsy word-order. To regale is 'to give delight to' here.

dame Lurch ... bandy children ... nor fasting, nor birch Note the choice of the name, implying unsteadiness, followed by deformity (the result of malnutrition), 'fasting' (ironic) and 'birch', to thrash the children with.

London

This superb poem has alternate lines rhyming in five quatrains which describe, with a fine economy of language and association, the degradation of contemporary life in the city, taking in disease and poverty, and particularly the 'marks of weakness, marks of woe'. The extent of human degradation is most fully conveyed in the second verse, and the third illustrates the social evils (the lot of the chimney sweeper and the soldier) which are condoned by the Church. The last verse returns to the theme of disease and even equates the marriage bed with a hearse; this poem is obviously an expression of complete physical and mental corruption. It is a moving and powerful poem, a savage indictment of what man has become and of man's desecration of man, but despite the savagery, perhaps even because of it, there is a quality of poignancy and compassion which is hard to ignore.

charter'd This means 'licensed' or give privileges to, and also a written grant of rights given by the sovereign or the legislature to a company: the repetition here is obviously ironic. A committee of the corporations of London had certain 'rights' with regard to the usage of the Thames.

mark ... Marks Again the deliberate repetition, the half-pun meaning 'note' on the one hand and 'evidence' or 'signs' on the other.

In every The insistent repetition of the poem underlines the dirge-like or wailing quality *and* the widespread degradation.

cry of fear Because the infant is threatened or beaten.

every ban The word means 'curse'.

mind-forg'd manacles i.e. chains made by the mind, which thus bind it, imprison it, so that it cannot admit enlightenment or humanity.

Chimney-sweeper's cry i.e. of pain.

black'ning church appalls The cry appalls the Church not because it pities the sweeps' lot but because the Church condones this social evil. A further pun is contained in the use of the word 'appalls', for a pall is a cloth used at funerals to spread over the coffin, hearse or tomb.

Runs in blood down Palace walls The idea is of the 'hapless' dying at the whim of Kings; it is a vivid image without specificity, but with the 'blood' of the French Revolution and England's colonial wars perhaps in mind.

Blasts Withers, blights.

plagues ... Marriage hearse A superb paradox, for hearses are used at funerals, not weddings. It seems to mean the horrors that the child will inherit in an evil world, as well as the curse of venereal disease.

The Human Abstract

This poem is in six quatrains, each having two rhyming couplets. It is a difficult poem, the title itself having been changed from that of *The Human Image*. In the first verse Blake shows how the virtues of mercy and pity presuppose the existence of poverty and suffering (an ideal life obviously would have no need of them). The second verse describes the uneasy peace based on fear, which in turn is followed by selfish love; cruelty then breeds grief, and humility, often seen as a virtue, is here expressed as something which comes about because of cruelty. The fourth verse defines mystery as a dismal shade (ignorance or darkness), and the 'Catterpiller and Fly', who represent religion in the form of the clergy, are those who feed on it. The image is one of stagnation, of nullity rather than life, and this gives rise to negations (of humanity) like tempting hypocrisy, or destructive appetite (the Raven). All natural forces have tried to identify the mystery, but it cannot be found in nature, for it exists only in the mind, and is a form of corruption. The personification runs throughout, and the emphasis is on the experience of the mind, how it corrupts, destroys, mutilates, and how abstract reasoning acts against 'nature'.

Pity ... Mercy Seen as attributes, qualities to be displayed in the human situation.

knits a snare i.e. constructs a trap.

Mystery The unknown, the origins.

the Catterpiller and Fly The religious sects, who make much out of the Mystery by analysis and explanation.

Deceit Hypocrisy. Notice that it has a 'fruit' – temptation – like the Tree of Knowledge in the Garden of Eden.

the Raven Symbolic of a destructive, lustful, predatory appetite.

The Gods of earth and sea i.e. nature.

this Tree Of 'abstract' speculation, the power of the mind.

Infant Sorrow

This was originally part of a longer poem, but it is an effective short whole here. The world which the child enters is seen as dangerous; 'like a fiend hid in a cloud' conveys the effect of the child being stifled/repressed, though some critics have felt that 'fiend', like 'tiger', represents 'natural instincts', here suppressed. The masterly second verse indicates a sulky acceptance after struggle, and we look back on *Infant Joy*, which, as its title suggests, is the complete 'contrary' to this poem, for here we find the sorrow of birth as distinct from the lyrical joy of its inception in the earlier poem.

Like a fiend hid in a cloud Blake's similes are frequently, as here, short and visually effective.

A Poison Tree

Psychologically this is a fascinating poem; it describes not one man's self-destruction but a fundamental human failing. The first verse sounds the ominous note through its reiterative pattern, and immediately 'anger' or 'hate' becomes the theme. The implication is that anger confessed destroys itself, but that hidden anger festers. This theme runs through the second verse; the underlying hatred is masked by a show of mock friendliness. This deception deludes the enemy, who is killed by the revelation of the poison which has been gathering head within and which destroys. But both speaker and foe are fallen: the speaker in his hypocrisy and the foe in his deceitful stealing into the garden at night. Because of the associations of the tree and the apple, we are in the apparent world of innocence (the Garden of Eden), but this proves to be the devastating world of experience (hate, hypocrisy, death). The effects are achieved through the repetition, the placing of 'glad' which gives an additional force to the poem, while the illustrations complement the text exquisitely.

water'd ... sunned Note the irony inherent in the contrast – water and sun foster growth, here unnatural growth.

an apple The symbol of temptation.

the night had veil'd the pole i.e. covered everything in blackness.

A Little Boy Lost

This poem consists of six verses and is written in the familiar quatrains with alternate lines rhyming in lines two and four. In the first two verses, the child suggests that self-love is the most natural form of love, and that man cannot know anything greater than man. This basic concept causes the priest – at once the representative of religion and repression – to indict the child before the 'altar high'. This is because he has dared to set 'reason up for judge'. The child is then stripped and burned, so that the poem is a symbolic narrative of the 'awakening mind' being subdued, stifled, crucified by the blind power of authority. Though allegorical, the poem has an immediate and horrific vividness, and the poet identifies himself with the individual (here a child) making a stand before authority, here personified by the priest in the name of religion. The use of the word 'lost' is doubly ironic; the child is 'lost' to reason and faith because he has displayed a basic power of reasoning. The unanswered question at the end of the final verse is sufficient indication of Blake's emphatic contemporary reference.

A greater than itself to know i.e. it is impossible for the human mind to conceive of the nature of God.

like the little bird/That picks up crumbs around the door This beautiful and simple image shows *real love* as distinct from the professed love (i.e. in faith).

trembling zeal i.e. angry enthusiasm.

the Priestly care Concern, but the poet's tone, unlike the onlookers' approbation, is ironic.

a fiend A devil, an agent of Satan.

holy Mystery i.e. God and the origins of creation and, later, of Christianity.

strip'd Stripped.

a holy place This last verse is bitterly ironic: it is a commonplace to speak of burning in hell.

Albion's shore The ancient name for Great Britain, meaning a 'white cliff'.

A Little Girl Lost

Probably a 'contrary' with *The Little Girl Lost* of *Innocence*. The first, italicized verse is addressed to the children of 'the Future Age'. The invocation to the future is the prelude to an allegory of the present, with the first verse proper dealing with the age of innocence (or the ideal age) in which a 'holy light' surrounds the youth and maiden in love. The third verse depicts the idyllic love which exists between them, a love which defeats fear. In the next verse the young people agree to meet to fulfil their love, but in the penultimate verse the girl goes to her father; his looks, derived from Biblical teaching of the sanctity of marriage – not love – fill her with fear. He speaks fearfully, believing that his daughter has sinned, and his whole attitude is one of reproach. Thus this girl is 'lost' before the coldness of the religious attitude and life, and is 'lost' also to the natural love which should be a joy to her. This is but a brief summary of a very important poem which exalts love and once again attacks attitudes which frustrate it, attitudes which disapprove and destroy. There is almost a catch in the voice in the fourth line of the italicized verse, and this reflects Blake's own loving concern.

Love! sweet Love! The exclamations underline Blake's sympathy.

Age of Gold i.e. the ideal age, innocence.

Naked in the sunny beams Free from constraint.

softest care i.e. sympathetic consideration.

holy light Note the repetition of the phrase, indicative of innocence.

soon forgot her fear Ona fears that her parents would disapprove of this meeting.

o'er heaven's deep At night.

white Indicating purity, but here of a rigorous, narrow kind.

Like the holy book Compare this with 'holy light' – the weight here is on Biblical authority.

Ona Probably Una, or the feminine form of 'one'.

pale and weak i.e. sinful.

To Tirzah (probably added about 1801)

This differs in tone from the other songs, though the four quatrains are in rhyming couplets. Tirzah represents the maker of the physical body, 'Thou Mother of my Mortal part' (stanza 3). In the first verse Blake quotes Christ's words to his mother at Cana 'then what have I to do with thee?' to convey the bodily and spiritual constrictions placed on man. The second, superbly condensed, deals with the association of sexuality and shame, the Fall of Man, who is saved by God's mercy and rises to work and to suffer and to repent. The third verse is an account, somewhat fierce, of motherhood and of the impositions placed on the child, while the fourth verse moves from the confines of mortality which are only transcended by the 'Death of Jesus' and the spiritual life. The focus on the life of the spirit is clear from the inscription on the illustration, 'It is raised a spiritual body'.

To rise from Generation free 'Mortal Birth' and 'generation' confine and imprison man; only by casting aside Tirzah can man be free.

Blow'd in the morn i.e. blossomed in the morning (desire).

in evening died A reference to hearing the voice of God. See note, p. 36 (Genesis, 3,8).

But Mercy changed Death into Sleep Adam and Eve were not condemned to death but to 'sleep' – life.

to work and weep To work and to suffer (for they had sinned).

The Mother of my Mortal part Motherhood, symbolized as narrow constraint and possessiveness as the verse unfolds.

The Death of Jesus set me free i.e. because of His sacrifice, man is free to live both in the flesh and the spirit.

The School Boy

Like others of Blake's songs, the illustrations here are an interesting comment on the theme. They show three boys playing a game at the foot of a tree, while others are climbing what appears to be a vine, and another boy is sitting at the top with an open book. The schoolroom, and the process of education, are seen as destructive forces which strip the boy of his youthful innocence and joy. Unusually, there is a five-line verse with alternate lines rhyming, and the tone is almost conversational, the first verse being given over to the praise of nature; the second, in complete contrast to it, shows the boy having to attend school, he and his companions being therefore imprisoned for the rest of the day. The next two verses pursue the nature-boy comparisons, the boy being compared to a bird in a cage which cannot be expected to sing. The final two verses underline this in no uncertain terms, with the idea that nature stripped and maimed in spring does not grow through the summer into an autumn fullness. Consequently the analogy, finely put, is that the child must have the freedom to develop *naturally* and not be constricted by a claustrophobic education.

winds his horn i.e. sounds it by blowing.

a cruel eye outworn Almost an anticipation of a Dickensian caricature of a schoolmaster. 'Outworn' probably means 'exhausted', having no animation.

learning's bower An ironic description for 'abode, dwelling'.

with the dreary shower i.e. monotonous instruction (note the parallel with nature).

droop his tender wing The whole phrase is transferred, a continuation of the bird comparison.

O father & mother An invocation to the parents *not* to send
him to school.
nip'd Affected by the cold.
strip'd ... dismay i.e. laid bare to the anguish of those who
care for natural growth or development.
gather ... mellowing year i.e. in Autumn. Note how this
verse traces the cycle of nature.

The Voice of the Ancient Bard

This poem was at first included by Blake in the *Songs of
Innocence* but was later moved to *Songs of Experience*. It
is an uneven little poem, with the tone verging on the
conversational and the casual rhyming doing little to en-
hance the effect. Blake calls to the 'Youth of delight' to
tell him that the 'Image of truth' has arrived and the
conflicts of the past are over. Yet the second half of the
poem carries a certain ambiguity, for while the implication is that 'Folly' belongs to the past, Blake also suggests that it is a permanent part of human nature, while
the length and structure of the final lines seem to suggest
the continuity of it. It may be that the poem expresses
optimism and hope but that Blake is aware too of the
natural conflicts which beset achievement.

artful teazing i.e. cunning, malicious activity.
perplex her ways i.e. confuse.
but care/And wish Although they are ignorant, they still
foolishly pursue their wishes.

A Divine Image

This represents the 'contrary' to *The Divine Image* in
Songs of Innocence, the first verse here being a complete
reversal of the third verse of that poem. The second verse
here represents the twisted or ugly nature of man by taking
the last line of the first verse as a starting point (Human
Dress) and by working backwards through the verse to

underline the terror and power of man as distinct from the mercy and kindness, for example, of the earlier poem. The result is that *A Divine Image* – an image of God in man – is a cruel indictment of human nature and the powerful and evil God who fashioned it. In the first verse the three personified attributes of human nature are cruelty, jealousy and fear, the final line emphasizing the deceit in appearances. In the second verse the figurative language – imagery of the industrial revolution – is used to emphasize power and appetite in the flesh – Iron, Forge, Furnace, Gorge – the repetition conveying the insistent movement of the forge and the unchanging qualities of man.

Secrecy i.e. deceit, dishonesty.
forged ... fiery Forge ... Furnace Note the powerful alliterative effect of the 'f's' and 'g's', which contrast sharply with the softness which there should be in 'form' and 'face'.
Gorge i.e. internal throat, appetite.

Revision questions on Songs of Experience

1 Which of the *Songs of Experience* do you find most vivid and moving and why?

2 What facets of contemporary life does Blake attack in *Songs of Experience*?

3 Write an essay on Blake's use of imagery in any three of the *Songs of Experience*.

4 What do you find obscure in *Songs of Experience*? Write an essay in interpretation of any two of the 'difficult' poems.

5 Discuss Blake's use of dialogue in any three or four of the *Songs of Experience*.

General questions

1 Write an essay on Blake's use of simple language, referring to at least two poems from each series.

Note-form guideline answer

Obviously you have a free choice here. The examples given below refer to *The Chimney Sweeper* and *Holy Thursday* from *Innocence* and *The Sick Rose* and *A Poison Tree* from *Experience*. Whatever your choice is, comment on the vocabulary that Blake uses and/or simple comparisons or images. But be sure to say also that the simple language sometimes carries a complex meaning.

(a) Introduction   Ballad form and other forms which Blake uses means that complex words would be out of place. Brief background introduction to *Innocence* and *Experience* – the 'contraries'.

(b) *The Chimney Sweeper*   Refer particularly to the force of 'sold', the simple rhymes of weep, sweep, cheep, including internal rhyme, the conversational tone of the poem – the loaded use of colour (white) – the language of understatement – the background of man's inhumanity to child, done through direct and simple language and images.

(c) *Holy Thursday*   Longer lines but still easy language which captures the procession, the clear pictures and comparisons (note the use of white again), the Biblical associations through simple analogy. Now choose two or three of your quotes from the poem and demonstrate how they fit the essential pattern of simplicity.

(d) *The Sick Rose*   Superbly simple language and form, but here with a weight of meaning and association.

Two verses only but simple words replete with the ideas of the corruption of nature and man/woman. Show how effectively the simple vocabulary conveys evil, the disease within nature and human nature, in eight short lines.

(e) *The Poison Tree* Analyse closely as above, paying direct attention to the vocabulary – but note, too, the simple words used in repetition, and estimate their effect. What is the effect, for example, of the repetition of 'my' and 'and'?

(f) Conclusion Choose those words and images which seem to you best able to illustrate Blake's lyrical and loaded techniques of expression through simple language. Sum up through quotation and comparative reference.

2 In what ways is the word 'contrary' essential to our understanding of these poems? Again you should choose two or more poems from each series.

3 What part does nature play in the poems referred to in these notes?

4 Compare and contrast any *pairs* of poems in these series.

5 In what ways do these poems express a kind of reality? Quote in support of your views.

6 Write an essay on Blake's use of symbols in any four of these poems.

7 What qualities in these poems make you think of them as 'Songs'?

8 Write an essay on Blake's use of personification or alliteration in these poems.

9 What use does Blake make of repetition in these poems? What effects does he achieve?

10 Write an essay on a selection of these poems, saying whether you think they are poetic exercises or whether they are written with sincerity.

11 As far as you can judge from these poems, give Blake's views on either the church (*or* authority in religion) *or* on marriage *or* on sexuality *or* on the spiritual life.

12 By a close study of two poems from each section, say what you learn of life at the time Blake wrote these poems.

13 In what ways did a study of the illustrations help you to appreciate these poems?

14 In what ways are these poems visions? Refer to two or three poems in your answer.

15 What do you learn of Blake from these poems? Support your answer by direct reference to three or more poems.

Further reading

The Life of William Blake, Mona Wilson
Blake: Complete Writings, edited by Sir Geoffrey Keynes
William Blake: Selected Poems, edited by F. W. Bateson
William Blake, D. G. Gilham
William Blake: The Critical Heritage, edited by G. E. Bentley, Jr

Brodie's Notes

TITLES IN THE SERIES

Edward Albee	Who's Afraid of Virginia Woolf?
Jane Austen	Emma
Jane Austen	Mansfield Park
Jane Austen	Pride and Prejudice
Samuel Beckett	Waiting for Godot
William Blake	Songs of Innocence and Experience
Robert Bolt	A Man for All Seasons
Charlotte Brontë	Jane Eyre
Emily Brontë	Wuthering Heights
Geoffrey Chaucer	The Franklin's Tale
Geoffrey Chaucer	The Knight's Tale
Geoffrey Chaucer	The Miller's Tale
Geoffrey Chaucer	The Nun's Priest's Tale
Geoffrey Chaucer	The Pardoner's Prologue and Tale
Geoffrey Chaucer	Prologue to the Canterbury Tales
Geoffrey Chaucer	The Wife of Bath's Tale
Wilkie Collins	Woman in White
Joseph Conrad	Heart of Darkness
Charles Dickens	Great Expectations
Charles Dickens	Hard Times
Charles Dickens	Oliver Twist
Charles Dickens	A Tale of Two Cities
Gerald Durrell	My Family and Other Animals
George Eliot	Silas Marner
T. S. Eliot	Selected Poems
Henry Fielding	Tom Jones
F. Scott Fitzgerald	The Great Gatsby and Tender is the Night
E. M. Forster	Howard's End
E. M. Forster	A Passage to India
John Fowles	The French Lieutenant's Woman
Anne Frank	The Diary of Anne Frank
Mrs Gaskell	North and South
William Golding	Lord of the Flies
Graham Greene	Brighton Rock
Graham Greene	The Power and the Glory
Graham Handley (ed)	The Metaphysical Poets: John Donne to Henry Vaughan
Thomas Hardy	Far From the Madding Crowd
Thomas Hardy	The Mayor of Casterbridge
Thomas Hardy	The Return of the Native
Thomas Hardy	Tess of the D'Urbervilles
L. P. Hartley	The Go-Between
Aldous Huxley	Brave New World
James Joyce	Portrait of the Artist as a Young Man
John Keats	Selected Poems and Letters of John Keats
Philip Larkin	Selected Poems of Philip Larkin

ENGLISH COURSEWORK BOOKS